WORKBOOK

For

GIRL, STOP APOLOGIZING

A Shame-Free Plan for Embracing and Achieving Your Goals

Rachel Hollis

By

TIMELINE Publishers

ISBN: 978-1-951161-05-7

Legal Notice

This Book is Copyright protected. This Book is only for personal use. You cannot amend, distribute, sell, use, quote or paraphrase any part, or the content within this book, without the consent of the author or publisher.

Disclaimer Notice

This is a Workbook and Summary Review, not the Original book. Please note, the information contained within this document is for educational and entertainment purpose only. All effort has been executed to present accurate, up to date, and reliable, complete information. No warranties of any kind are declared or implied. Readers acknowledge that the author is not engaging in the rendering of legal, financial, medical or professional advice. The contained within this book has been derived from various sources

Table of Contents

How to Use this Workbook For Enhance Application

This book is written in a way that Complete beginners can use this *Workbook* ***for Girl,*** *Stop Apologizing:* ***A Shame-Free Plan for Embracing and Achieving Your Goals by Rachel Hollis to get immediate help from the major lessons and Summary of this book.***

The goal of this Workbook is to help even the newest of readers to apply major lessons from Girl, Stop Apologizing: A Shame-Free Plan for Embracing and Achieving Your Goals by Rachel Hollis. Results have shown that learning is retained better through repeated real-life applications

By using this Workbook, readers will find Summary and Lessons which we believed were major in defining the crucial messages of the author in the book.

There are Spaces to jot down your answers to lesson at the end of each Section. Take out a pencil, pen, or whatever digital technology you would put to use to jot down, implement, and follow the guide appropriately.

And don't forget to have fun – While at it. This Workbook Will aid you acquire skilld in your path to growth, confidence, and believing in yourself.

The Background Story of Girl, Stop Apologizing

Rachel Hollis is an admirable personality who started her career as an event planner now turned entrepreneur. She is notable for her lifestyle blog named *TheChicite.com* amongst other outstanding feats; top podcast host, CCO of The Hollis Company, a TV personality, bestselling author on different platforms as she attained New York Times best-selling author of *Girl, Wash Your Face,* showcased by Inc. Magazine as one of the *"Top 30 Entrepreneurs under 30"* in 2009, she's been married for 11 years and blessed with a supportive husband David Hollis and is mother to 3 sons and a daughter.

She studied American Academy of Dramatic Arts in Los Angeles; ans was born on 9th January 1983 in California, United States. Rachel Hollis has other fictional book series to her name called *The Girls* and cookbook recipes exploring her culinary interest. Her motivational speaking has touched the lives of many women all over the world.

INTRODUCTION

What if?

Being you and not being sorry for it is not bitchy, but what I term the “new sexy”. In fact, the day you cease to seek peoples’ opinion or expectations as it pertains to your dream, lifestyle, goals, and aspiration is the day you start to live life to its fullest. This is not to mean that you rudely or bitterly cajole anyone to toll the line of your school of thought /beliefs, but focus on your dream, work on making it a masterpiece and stop feeling guilty about it. Too many questions have limited many women today, questions are not meant to negatively affect us, but we are humans and we are susceptive and cannot do without pondering over things in our heart.

Where there is cause for concern is when it is combined with fear, only then will the faith she took days to build come crumbling down in seconds. This is because there was the seed of doubt lingering somewhere from the very beginning, so she concludes that her goals will fail before it even starts and this mindset needs to be discarded if we are to change our world and it starts with you. Too many "what ifs" have moved our focus from our goals, and have truncated the colossal and positive world change that would bring about a revolution which would affect our live’s, that of our friends, the community, and the world at large and cause it to out-live many generations.

Truth be told, women are scared of themselves. If not, I don’t see why we devote so much of our time to express regret always for who we are or what we want out of life, instead of combining that energy to chase both. Societal norms are good, it molds us to be presentable and better accepted as we function in the various facet of the society, but does not determine who we are and should not change our originality and how we view life.

Yes, our background can serve as a blueprint of how we face situations, how we tackle challenges, our dependency level, confidence level and much more… But it shouldn't stop there, grow up and out of being spoon-fed, take up the challenges you are faced with and achieve a new feat every now and then and stop looking for approval or permission as to if you should chase your dreams or not in other not to hurt your family and friends, so they don't call you selfish, greedy or self-absorbed when in the real sense of the whole fracas; you are achieving your dreams and getting the win you've worked so hard to achieve which means when you win they all have won equally and their lives will be affected positively.

Get out from that couch of excuses that you have been stuck to for so long and surge forward by adopting the required skill and habit that can help you grow and succeed no matter how small. Make sure to leave behind the lies and fear of failing. Set big goals and aim to achieve them personally and professionally.

1. *What are the areas in your life you are unapologetic for?*

____

____

____

____

____

____

____

____

____

____

2. *What are your fears in life as it pertains to your career and personal life?*

____

3. *Why do you term yourself a failure?*

PART I: EXCUSES TO LET GO OF

What are excuses?

Excuses are a conscious attempt to defend and justify an act in an attempt to lessen the blame attached to the subject matter. In most cases, excuses are believed and serves as a platform not to achieve set goals which leads to hopelessness and a consciousness that ones dreams can not be attained before it even began. This has to end, below are possible excuses we often give that holds us back from achieving our goal.

Excuse 1. That's Not What Other Women Do

Perfectionism has always been a thorn in the flesh for many people and seeing others do something in a certain way that happens not to be the way you would have done it, automatically means your process was wrong after all. We hate the way we look, smell, talk, smile, dress, speak, eat, walk, think, and generally appear because that is not the way the other women do it. Tell me, what makes the opinion of other women superior to yours? Why do you feel you are the one who is different and can't fit in? In a world where things work right, pressure from peers or the society shouldn't make one change their personality but help to groom, encourage, refine these attributes, and gain a strong self-confidence knowing that you are not an outcast or an alien because you are different from the others.

Unfortunately, our society does not present these opportunities every day; we grew up taking conscious notes of what we lacked in our features, we have been told that we are too fat, too tall, too thin, too big, too black, very ugly and will therefore not be accepted or loved. Some women get to handle these sorts of remarks well, while others are drowned by it. We do a very good job with living the lives of other women even though we hate the choices we are making just to gain acceptance, and going back on these choices can be very difficult especially when you have fallen too deep and cannot go back. Many people are living dual lives and many will live dual lives all through their time on earth because they have failed to accept who they are. Start loving you, praise yourself when you achieve a feat and don't bury every accomplishment, stop downplaying your impact and how you have positively affected your immediate world, say to yourself that you have done well and admit your biggest dreams to yourself. Stop worrying about what will be said about you and if people out there will get the original intent of towing the lane you did and the gains. You have so much to give! Stop hiding behind that curtain, talents, and skills has life and they cannot grow in the dark. So, come out and impact other women, change their thinking, school of thought, orientations, mental health and boost their downtrodden self-esteem. I know this is not easy; there are mean people who will say terrible and horrible things about you, they will pour their frustration and hate on you and think of you as they view themselves and how they feel the world should be, but you have to be determined and grow a thicker skin to withstand them all. Keep at feeding your drive, nurture your dream consistently and soon you will stop being the subject of discussion but you will be discussion itself.

It's not a walk in the park; it requires hard work and patience to get the best out of any venture, so it's not when it gets too difficult and stressful that you give-up; but the set time to double your hustle and make a point that you know what you stand for and you are unapologetically proud of it. How long are you going to be ashamed of what you do? How long are you going to go on living your life to please others? How will you go with this weight of perfectionism on your shoulder? How long will your life be determined successful or not by people's expectation of you? How long will others determine your value and worth?

We have been trained to know and identify the huge difference between the way females should be and the way the males should be. This is not a subject of feminism; the crux of the matter is to re-address who boys and girls are raised to be and how they view life. Many women grew up believing that, a good woman is that one who is only good for other people thereby damaging your self-worth. No wonder today we have many women walking about not knowing if they are worth much or anything at all, so it is easy to sway these ones with any wind of doctrine. You have your value intact with or without the positive opinion of others, don't be deceived.

LESSON

Stop going by what others think is best for you, start living your life for you. What do you want out of life? People can advise you, but that should not form a basis for your entire life. Live your life, it's yours and only you can truly account for it when the time comes. Waste no more time and get to work on yourself.

1. *What are the excuses you have believed overtime that has limited you?*

____

____

____

____

____

____

____

2. *How is your background affecting who you are today and how you view life?*

3. *What choices have you made that you wish you can go back on?*

4. *What do you feel guilty for or ashamed of and sorry for?*

5. *What has been your long-life dream, your limitations to achieving them and have you been able to attain any?*

Excuse 2: I'm Not A Goal-Oriented Person

This is another excuse many of us give to evade the truth about ourselves. It's wrong to agree that you are no good and not goal-oriented or do not have anything to live for. No one came into this world with a skillset, you didn't come into the world knowing how to drive, or how to bake a cake, or knowing the workings of your system. There are no inborn traits and it requires daily grooming to be perfect. Likewise getting healthy habits that will benefit your life. How can one even function without setting goals and aspiration to achieve per time? Be a goal digger, always set new goals for you after surmounting the last.

Learn new skills, find your goal, focus on it and learn at working on it to get closer to your dreams daily. Dreams vary as it pertains to our backgrounds but they generally are things you hope, yet to be seen in your life but serves a constant reminder of your focus and a valid reason to keep working at it but it is not a strategy. Yes! You may feel you are not goal-oriented or have a drive that keeps you going, but you must definitely want something, everyone wants something out of life. The only difference is that while others can defend, project and proudly showcase their hopes and dreams for life; others who equally have goals has chosen to be mute and have accepted whatever Life throws at them.

In as much as everyone has goals and hopes, they are not the same. Goals are dreams that need to be worked on in other for it to be materialized. It is a destination you are working to and not an idea you hope to make real tomorrow. While hope is an important tool that keeps you motivated about the future and over time can help bring your dreams to actualization. Hope without adopting active steps, in reality, is a futile journey. Having goals and achieving feats gives you a sense of purpose, responsibility, accomplishment and leaves you happy. Start with putting down your goal, ask yourself - who do I want to be? And figure out how to take positive steps to actualize your goal.

You are a woman with value and you are permitted to have dreams and goals. Get to work today and remember every single thing living (businesses, relationship, organisms) either grows or dies.

LESSON

Having goals and achieving feats gives you a sense of purpose, responsibility, accomplishment, and leaves you happy. Start with putting down your goals, ask yourself - who do I want to be? And figure out how to take positive steps to actualize your goal.

1. *What are your career / personal dreams?*

____

____

____

____

____

____

____

____

____

____

____

____

2. *Will you describe yourself as a goal-oriented woman and how do you know you are?*

3. *What are your goals, how will you go about achieving them and how long will it take to achieve them?*

4. *What are the habits you need to adopt to become the self-fulfilled woman you want to be?*

Excuse 3: I Don't Have Time

This is often a common excuse we give; we say we are occupied and that our schedules are filled up. The truth is, there really comes a time in our lives where there won't be time available to do those things you love. Every passing day comes with an additional responsibility on your shoulders and with time you will make your goal second-fiddle and you take up a totally different path that pacifies the present situation.

Yes, your present schedule is overwhelming already and seems like there is no space for your goals to thrive. But in the real sense, it can be compromised and none of the parties in question will suffer. This is not about finding time to pursue your dreams because you will never find the time, what you are going to do is to create time from all the frenzy and give those God-given goals resident inside of you an opportunity to glow.

No one has full control of your time except you, regardless of how demanding the events surrounding your life gets you have to begin to believe this. So you see; you have been the one depriving yourself all along. You cannot make headway if you keep repeating the mistakes of yesterday if you want things to change around you; start with the change. Drop everything limiting you if it's a habit; end it and move forward. Have it at the back of your mind that in other to progress a lot of trading will take place, you will give-up going to the cinema every Fridays to nurture your dream, or your frequent outings with friends or unnecessary strolls in the park to make new friends... All of these and more chokes your schedule and makes achieving your goal unrealistic.

LESSON

Time is sacred and should be treated as such. Anytime wasted can never be earned back, so why waste your precious time. With that out of the way, it is wise to get a note (mental notes can fail) where you record how you spend your time every day of the week. After a week's assessment, you should be able to see where to add your goal-achieving time to in the entire schedule and stick to it.

This whole process of tracking your daily activity will not make sense if you don't treat your time sacred. In time you wouldn't have any need for the notepad; you'll just mentally know what you have to do per hour. This doesn't only help you keep track of how you spent your time or what you spent your time doing, but it helps you respect and value time better. Repeat a workable schedule every week in line with your mental capacity and always make the best of your skill acquiring time.

1. *What value do you place on your time?*

____

____

____

____

____

____

2. *What takes up most of your time and debars you from achieving your goal?*

3. *What are the new things you want accomplished in your life?*

4. *What are the plans you will establish today to take you closer to your goals?*

Excuse 4: I'm Not Good Enough To Succeed

Have you signed up to fail before you ever attempt to succeed?

Feelings of uncertainty are another enemy to the human mind. You feel you cannot succeed and will fail in that endeavor. I'm Not Good enough to succeed syndrome affects a lot of us. You say you are not good enough for her because you are yet to be as wealthy as expected by the society, you feel you are not pretty enough to get married, you feel you can't make it to the finish line of the race as an athlete before the race even started.

For the fact that you are yet to get to where you want to be doesn't mean you will not get there eventually. Why are we scared of failing? When you learned to walk as a toddler, you fell down a couple of times and got hurt but you didn't stay down and you got right back up. Same goes for situations in life when you fall you might get hurt but you have to get up again. With repeated failures, you become aware of your flaws, where you went wrong, what you need to correct and then you become an enviable master at your craft. If you feel you are devoid of some attributes which had limited your level of success, then get to work on it and fill it up with the skills and virtues you want as a part of your life.

After identifying the problem, in attempting to get it fixed don't attempt to do what a friend or family did that worked for him because it might not work for you. Everyone and their cases are peculiar, just the way no two pregnancies carried by the same mother is the same. Find what works for you and stick to it, personal growth is personal.

LESSON

Dear, you are just enough for you. How long will you look down on yourself? End the self-battery and accord yourself some accolade. It is not a crime to be at the starting point, but it becomes a crime when you dwell there far too long. Whenever that silly feeling arises that you are not good enough, silence it with the truth and not your opinion that is inspired by what people think of you.

1. *What wrong impressions have you made-up for yourself that you need to change?*

____

____

____

____

____

____

____

2. *What do you see in others that you feel you lack and has limited you thus far?*

____

____

____

____

____

____

____

3. *Give yourself some credit for the things you have accomplished and the list of things you are yet to accomplish?*

4. *Can you attempt writing a letter to yourself, from yourself? (Make sure to write from the part of you that never gave up and represents the opposite of your fears)*

Excuse 5: I Can't Pursue My Dream And Still Be A Good Mom/Daughter/Employee...

Fill in the blank space you happen to occupy at the moment, but not for long because I am hoping you'll all have a change after reading.

Women are the human species known to multi-task the best. A woman can be a mum, an entrepreneur and an employee all at the same time and still pursue her dreams. Over the years, the norms of how we grew up and the attachments that come with it limit us from moving forward in life. Family pressure, societal pressure and other forms of pressure drowns one and then you let go of your initial vision and focus. This has been so for far too long because they matter more and their happiness is a priority and not yours. This is not to rudely say you don't care about your family and immediate society, or that the intention of all I have been saying since is to groom selfish women all over the world who care less about any other person. The aim here is to remind women to live for themselves as well as for others.

You can have a successful but unbalanced work-life relationship (the scale can never be balanced). Many women feel this is a myth but haven't attempted giving it a try or asking for help on how to. There will always be an endless battle between work and personal life as each of them tries to be superior to the other and both want equal attention. It's not a bad thing because that's just how the world is wired. Here is another sad reality; you have done very well as a great family member, colleague, and friend. But you have the right to focus on your goals and this will mean missing out some time with your loved ones for a greater good. It's the sacrifice you have to pay to attain your dreams.

To be honest, what tops my chart is a priority and will, therefore, require more of my attention. Our goal should be to be centered and not balanced. Being centered makes your mind settled and at peace with oneself. Still doing everything you need to do as it concerns your entire life (job, marriage, parenting, social life, family) and making everything just flow simultaneously into the other in a smooth synergy.

LESSON

Tell yourself, "I can get to fulfill my obligations as a mother, aunt, sister, daughter, employee, employer, entrepreneur and still get to achieve all my dreams and goals. At the end of the day, I am the only one who gets to decide what is true for me.

1. *What do you understand by work-life balance?*

____

____

____

____

____

____

____

2. *Have you been able to ever successfully strike a balance in your job and family?*

____

____

____

____

____

____

____

3. *If you have ever been able to do the above successfully, kindly tell me about it?*

____

____

____

____

____

____

____

____

4. Which will you say is the bigger challenge; your job or the home front and why?

____

____

____

____

____

____

____

Excuse 6: I'm Terrified Of Failure

The first few minutes when an idea or dream drops in your heart, thousands of positive thoughts cloud your mind on ways to carry it out and bring in to limelight. But quietly, the "WHAT IF'S" starts sipping through, and turns all your hopes and faith to doubts.

It just takes one minute to be positive and the next to be negative about the same idea you were ecstatic about earlier. The "WHAT IF'S" are not totally bad, in fact, they serve as a check to weigh the situations surrounding the dream and can help to choose the feasible of them. When it becomes evil is when the "WHAT IF'S" cause us to draw back in your shell and lock away the dreams from seeing the sun.

There is no point lying about the evident truth. Getting up after failing isn't fun at all. Many people dread attempting to give their dreams a chance because they cannot stand the hurts of failure. Don't be afraid to fail, because only then will you learn and devise better ways of achieving your dreams. With your mistakes, you become a better you. Don't be ashamed of falling, its best you even get to fall in the early stages so that you later become a lord in that same field.

LESSON

You are not permitted to be afraid of failing, what you should be afraid of is never getting to achieve anything because you were very scared of what others might think of you for giving your dream a try.

1. *Have you ever attempted trying out your dreams and how did it go?*

____

____

____

____

____

____

____

____

____

____

2. *When you failed at achieving your dreams what were the measures you adopted to bring you back up without being ashamed?*

____

____

____

____

____

____

____

3. *What Spiral did your recent failure episode take, did it make you a better person or left you worse?*

Excuse 7: It's Been Done Before

This is one of those things we do very well. We pull back on attaining what we want because someone else is already doing it or has done it before. Why do we wear trending clothes, designers, shoes, bags, phones... when they all have been bought, worn and used by millions of people and many more people believing God to have materialistic items like that someday. We fail to accord this same pursuit when it comes to pursuing our goals. And then we provide a good excuse to follow suite.

Let go of these excuses, even if someone has already done what you have dreamed of means you are equally creative and not as a competition. You don't have to be scared and decide to drop off the race because you feel you don't stand a chance and will never be a good as she is. The person you are intimidated about didn't become like this overnight, much work has gone into the process of making that fine gold you cherish.

You will get your fingers burnt, you will step on terrains you have never known in your life but it is all about the learning process and you will also come out stronger, well-refined, sturdy, confident, and vast in your field. It will take some time to master this, but it will definitely happen.

LESSON

No matter how saturated your industry is, you should be able to carve a niche for yourself and still have your name on the lips of many. As I always say, the sky is very large for every single star to have its place comfortably. Challenges don't end, as you progress in life, there is one mountain to level and another and another and it goes on and one; so don't get tired or scared just yet.

1. *What are your dreams and does it fall in the same situation discussed above?*

____

____

____

____

____

____

____

____

____

2. *Share your experience with me and how you surmounted it*

____

____

____

____

3. *Will you say rivalry is a strong motivator for achieving success?*

Excuse 8: What Will They Think?

You are lost when the expectations of people determines how you act or treat others around you.

Having people at the back of your mind at all times and pondering what their opinion is about your dream is a limiting factor. Stop looking out for what people think of you because you are fueling their opinion and giving them the power to order your life.

People can advise you, but there is a wide disparity to needing that person's approval or opinion. It is absolutely wrong to build your world around their perception of you. What will you tell those who look up to you, can you confidently tell them that you have been living your life by the leading and opinion of someone who knows nothing about you? And those innocent ones that see you a mentor have been adopting lifestyle built on lies and deceit...

When people have an opinion about you, it is either hearsay or validated. What is the intention of that information? Is it to make you a better person or act as a stinger? Also, who is the person presenting this info to you, is it a family member, a friend or a stranger? This can be the deciding factor in accepting or trashing that advice. This will help you know the place the person is coming from, you will perceive it to be thoughtful, kind, caring and genuinely concerned.

LESSON

We can conclude that we will only move forward when we bother less on what others think about us and more about what we think of ourselves. Only you can give power to people's opinion about you. Start to be intentional about living henceforth. Take active steps towards this cause and start living the free life.

1. Have you ever felt stuck under the burden of others opinions and expectations and who do they happen to be?

2. What level will you say does people's perception about you affect your life?

3. Have you ever been able to deal with a perception issue?

Excuse 9: Good Girls Don't Hustle

Growing up, our parents started imbibing in us that as females there is a lot we can and cannot do. While on the other hand the male children were time and again cajoled to strive very hard to achieve more out of life. It's not a crime to want more from life regardless of your social status or background. It's not out of place to want power, influence and wealth as a woman although our society terms it improper but welcomes it for the male folks.

I get tired of the status quo and set new goals for myself. I am never comfortable in any situation, there can be better. Don't be happy with whatever life throws at you. Seek new experiences, challenges, broaden your horizon and surpass new feats. Live life to the fullest, be everything and anything you want to be, don't let any limitations hold you back, only you have the power to change your life.

LESSON

Don't downplay your aspirations or intimidating goals because the world sees it as uncomfortable. We need to start taking the good out of every situation and drawback on the negatives. If a woman's goal triggers you to write down yours and set up measures to help you achieve them, why not? Take the big leap and be who you want to be unapologetically. Tomorrow you will join the squad of women who you once looked up to and who cared more about changing the world than the opinion others had about you because you'll be busy impacting nations positively.

1. *Do you want more out of life?*

2. *What is your thought on girl power and the urge to want more than the norm*

PART II: BEHAVIORS TO ADOPT

Your behavior is simply the way you react to situations, whether good or bad. Your behavior displays what you are, thought patterns, what you say and generally how you live your life. Your behavior is your habit; many habits we pick up either have a positive or negative impact on our behavior, we need to be careful of the habits we unconsciously inherit because they can form a foundation and inform your entire goal setting process.

Behavior 1: Stop Asking for Permission

Not many are comfortable with the term *Feminist.* But it isn't as bad as it's acclaimed; feminism has to do with accepting that men and women should be treated equally and that they both have equal rights. This is not a male versus female sermon and should not be treated as such.

The truth is that whether consciously or unconsciously, many have adopted patriarchal as a bedrock to run their homes. Women are still looked down on, men feel it's not appropriate for a woman to drive a luxurious car, own a multimillion-dollar business, and become the president of a world country... It is strange and painful that even the right to cast our votes and make our opinion known was denied us some many years ago. As much as we will love to hide these facts and not want to talk about them, they exist.

Men have been idolized as a symbol of authority in most homes today. And it is passes on and on. From being a boy to a man who gets married and continues to preside over his house and various committees he represents. For some lucky women, the man may have her interest at heart and exercise his authority to making her a better person; what happens to those that are unfortunate to be with the bad ones? Imagine what hell they will be living in! This means that the men know best and have absolute authority, power, and control over all. They make all the decisions, they are in charge and greatly affect your life. But this is not our focus of discussion today, the most important thing is to be able to pull yourself out of the mess your immediate society and the world at large has made you believe about yourself as a woman and regain faith.

Even as a woman, you have the right and authority to chase your dreams without seeking the permission of a "Voice/symbol of authority". Even as wives, because of the way we were trained to seek daddy's approval at all times, we pass this down to our husbands. Just the way you always love to please your Dad and your mood is affected when Daddy's mood is awful, so will be the case in your marriage. You will never be able to live dependent on your own feelings which are abnormal.

You realize that you have spent over half of your years on Earth trying to please others most, making decisions based on what they would like to hear and not what is right for you. You need to stop seeking permission at all time and just do what you want to do.

This is what happens when you stop taking permission and own your life. You manage your responsibility, your priorities, your dream, goals and aspiration, and still are a great part of your relationship with the one you love, Friend and family members. Grown women don't seek permission; you are allowed to be the best you can be even if it inconveniences anyone.

There is a wrong notion that needs correcting. The term "Boss-girl". Qualifying something gives it limits, so to qualify the term above is disrespectful to us as women. This has gone on for too long; even women themselves don't know how damaging this is to our fight for equality in the business world. Somehow they are right to inspire the younger generation to cajole them that they can achieve greater things in life. The name-tagging needs to stop and be accorded more respect.

When a man makes it, it is seen as a normal feat. But when a woman does same, it surprises the world and we are named the girl-engineer, girl-physician, girl-nurse, girl-astronaut... Why should that be? Are we not human beings too? Why is it strange for us to achieve equal or even higher success than the other gender? Where is it written that women cannot be great or greater? Women, let's stop promoting this "Boss-girl" rubbish.

LESSONS

You don't need anyone's permission to be yourself. Neither do you need to reform your dreams to make it look sumptuous or acceptable? Be the woman you will be proud of, be the type of woman who will never ask for permission to be herself.

1. *Did you face any gender inequality while growing up?*

____

____

____

____

____

____

2. How did you face it and has if formed a better you today?

3. *What do you wish can be corrected about the subject matter as it concerns male and female upbringing?*

Behavior 2: Choose One Dream And Go All In

Have you ever heard of "Jack of all trade, master of none"? That's what this segment is about. To have a successful ride towards achieving your dreams, you need to focus on one per time. Use your daily activity as a case study, imagine you are watching the kids, doing the laundry, making dinner and trying to finish up your academic or work project all at the same time, how productive will you be? I know many will say they are very good at multi-tasking, but to say the truth; a divided attention cannot get the best out of an endeavor.

Some of us even try to beautify the situation and say that each of their dreams compliments the other, but still, it will not be effective all the same. Let's understand the difference between a dream and a cool idea. A dream is a desire imagined that is worth manifesting physically and made part of your everyday living. On the other hand, these cool ideas you have listed are part of your dreams but there will always be that one you will leave behind in the list for those ones that causes butterflies in your belly. Now that is your dream. Identify it and run with it with everything you have got.

The mistake most of us are making is that we choke our dream with awesome ideas. And then let our dream suffer, after all we then notice we cannot accomplish the dream, we throw in the towel and say it wasn't what they truly wanted for themselves in the first place. Going all in into achieving your dream means you are prepared to face it all come what may. Achieve one goal then proceed to the next. It's just like a growing child, she first learns to sit, and then crawl, and then walk and falls a lot of times before her feet become very strong.

The child didn't do all these at the same time, the gradual process of growth helped her know her terrain well, makes her comfortable in her body and know how to balance her weight on her legs... I cannot overemphasize the benefits of fully focusing on one dream per time, not only will the positive result come; but it will show up on time.

LESSON

Ever heard of the saying that it is better to master a craft ten times than to master 10 different crafts in the same space of time. The one who has mastered that 1 craft ten times over will definitely be a lord in his field and will be far better than the other who is learning 10 different crafts 10 times. When your focus is grounded on one thing, you will discover with time that other areas of your life grow along with it. It will always have a ripple effect, so change today and focus on just one dream, and achieve that one goal you have always desired.

1. *Have you ever been able to successfully separate your dreams from your ideas?*

____

____

____

____

____

____

2. *How do you measure your goal and your awesome ideas?*

3. *What do you need to change about your life and dreams to have the result you desire?*

4. *Do you think that focusing on only one of your dreams per time is a great idea for your personal growth and professional growth?*

Behavior 3: Embrace Your Ambition

Ambition is not an evil thing. Looking at its definition, "Ambition is a strong craving to do or to accomplish a thing, typically needing a strong resolve and hard work."

Ambition has no dangers or pitfalls when its in the right direction and focus. Now, this is also to say that ambition can be said to be dangerous. Imagine a workaholic with a great ambition, she will deny herself due rest, may forget to eat right many times; will forget to take her routine exercise daily which is unhealthy but because of what is ahead of her she is ready to take some risk and go the little extra. Now that's the kind of dangerous I can take but to generally refer to ambition as a dangerous venture for women is inappropriate.

This is not directed to spite men, but ladies sit for a second and think about this. Why is it acceptable and glorifying for men to be allowed to be ambitious and considered an asset when he updates his career? Why is it okay for men to learn more, improve their craft, and grow more? And it's not okay for women too? We need to stop this notion that certain rules only apply to a particular group of people who are in a certain stage of life.

LESSON

As a woman, wanting more than what you have attained so far is noteworthy and you should embrace it warmly. Do you want to learn more about your job? Do you want to acquire a new skill? Do you desire to take up a new course? Do you want to further your education to Ph.D. level? Go for it girl, don't let anything hinder you while you are at it. No level of segmentation should hold you back, even if it is coming from your immediate family, friends, or community. I always say that only YOU can stop YOU.

1. *In your opinion, do you feel that being ambitious is a bad thing as a woman?*

____

____

____

____

____

____

____

2. *Have you ever bothered that people see you attaining your dream and see you as ambitious?*

____

____

____

____

____

____

3. *Remembering that ambition causes you to stand out and be positively different from the others; are you ready to walk through the ambitious terrain and what is your driving force?*

Behavior 4: Ask For Help!

No one is an island, so; ask for some help. Everything we have spoken about isn't a walk in the park. It takes time to starts seeing the visible effects all these will have in your life. When you get stuck, when it getting very convoluted, when it gets all mixed up in itself, when it all looks unattainable, when you are about to throw in the towel; ask for some help.

A typical example will be to ask a nanny to help look after your kids as you get fired up to take on your ambition. It's not just about leaping into your ambition, you need to sit down and draw out how you intend to go about it in order not to crumble other aspects of your life. As I mentioned earlier, attaining your dreams is all about sacrifices. As you go about fulfilling those desires, who is helping to cover up for those aspects of your life that needs your attention. It's simple, just ask for help. As a working mum, You need the help of a caregiver to look after the kids when you are busy, she will help clean, cook, replace the groceries, put them to sleep and make sure the home is appealing to come back to while you are busy expanding your business overseas.

If you don't take proper care of this aspect, it will ruin your journey to greatness. Don't let anyone lie to you; everyone needs to help one way or another to be the best they can be. Many media portrays the well painted misleading perfect live in magazines, reality TV shows, soap operas, social media... Even media moguls who come up to say we can do it all, gain it all, be everything we want if we only work harder has left out a very important aspects of the speech which is, "ASK FOR HELP"! in their own lives, in other for them to attend the number of world occasions they do, socialites parties, presidential meetings etc. Some people are back home taking good care of their kids, the house manager, chef, engineer, gardener, and driver are performing their duties. These socialites cannot possibly live to their fullest aspirations without the help of these other guys back home. No matter how they paint it, these lives don't exist they are only fallacies. Be thankful for everyone who has helped you while you were busy chasing your career because without them it wouldn't have been possible.

There is another fallacy all over the internet and even in the lips of many women today. I am self-made. No one is fully self-made. Didn't it take the help of your family members, nannies, friends, husband... to help keep your family together while you were away conquering the world on your several business trips? So, why will anyone say they are self-made?

Getting help can be costly too, but you can start with getting help from a friend, spouse, neighbor, mother, sister till you can find your feet. Don't struggle alone please; you can't do this without help both emotionally and otherwise. You are permitted to struggle but it doesn't mean you are weak; it means you are human. Stop the pretense and ask for help, you will get one.

LESSON

There is nothing to be ashamed of asking for assistance. When you need to be ashamed is when you let your ego have its way by refusing to ask for help and your whole world comes crumbling down because you decided to climb up the ladder with 5 things on both arms and you have lost it all.

1. *Do you struggle to admit that you need help and why do you think that is so?*

____
____
____
____
____
____
____
____

2. *How comfortable are you with others helping you as you attain your goals?*

____
____
____
____
____

3. *Have you had any experience with a caregiver who took advantage of your absence to your disadvantage?*

4. *Would you rather not ask for help and let your dreams and home front suffer and why?*

Behavior 5: Build Foundations For Success

Building a solid foundation for the success you aim to attain is very vital. It's one thing to be motivated and another to have the enabling foundation to keep your goals alive. How is your schedule? Does it avail you the opportunity to thrive in the pursuit of attaining your goals? Lack of a structure to build on will not allow your dreams to go far. It's not rocket science, its basic fact. Imagine building a house without a foundation? That house can never stand the test of time, just a little wind and it is back on the ground. Here, the owner of the house has not only wasted time but resources and manpower gone down the drain.

Below are some of the imperative but easily downplayed things we need to put in place before embarking on pursuing our dreams.

1. **Take your health seriously**. Only a person who is physically and emotionally sound can work on their dreams. It's just like driving with a flat tire, how long can you really go with that? Eat healthy foods; know your body and what works for it. Shed excess weight, look great and get your body and soul together. Form the habit of drinking water, it's a great way to detoxify naturally and it is great for your body.

   Wake up early every day and start your day as an achiever that you are. You get a lot more achieved when you wake up early and face the business of the day. You can afford to work out, make breakfast without running up and down doing other additional chores and then go about your dreams.

Give up one unhealthy category of food for thirty days, Fast food precisely. I'm saying 30days because there is a saying that when you give up something for a month, there is a high tendency it will become a habit. Do this for yourself, replace that unhealthy option with a healthy one and keep your word.

Take exercise more seriously, at least 30 mins every day. Have you noticed that of all the animals in the forest, none is ever termed overweight because there is no overweight animal in nature? Only those who live in houses with us, they are pets. You are not a pet but a graceful, radiant, dashing, powerful, bold woman and you should begin to treat yourself as such.

Adopt the lifestyle of gratitude. Always look for every avenue to be thankful for your blessings no matter how supposedly insignificant they might be, the bottom line is; if you make it a habit to spend your day looking for blessing, it will find you out. This helps you build a positive mindset, and then over time, you become very optimistic about life in general.

2. **Get control of your personal space and keep it together.** Organize your life, no matter how little your space is, put it together. It starts with your home, how arranged is your home, your home is a reflection of your thoughts and the troubles, uncertainty or serenity in your heart. Keep your personal space clean and orderly.

3. **Build a great community.** We are all a perfect blend of the people we are closest to in this life. Pause for a minute and ponder on this. Who are your close pals? Which people do you talk and listen to frequently? Are some of them older than you and you have identified traits and skills you will love to adopt and aspire to be like them in future? That's a good place to be. But if you are the most intelligent amongst your friends, you are in the wrong place. Or you are the top goal-getter in your team? Get up and leave that room now! Surround yourself with individuals who are better than you in the parts you want development, people who are constantly learning one new thing daily.

4. **Cultivate great habits.** You have to quit habits that bring out the worst in you. Pick up those things that will aid your goal and work at it. It doesn't kick start in a day, but gradually it will pay off.

5. **Start a morning routine.** This is very important in our daily lives as achievers. What do you want to achieved today? As soon as you wake up early, write them down. This will direct your focus as you achieve them as the day goes by. Don't play with the routine; it has helped many to become great people we all aspire to be like today.

LESSONS

Women have lived their entire lives looking after others and no one to do the same for them. We use up so much energy trying to take care of others that we harm ourselves in the process. Though it is in our nature to care, in fact, we cannot function properly if we stop to care. So, it's okay to be tired, worn-out or anxious, you are going through the process and breaking down is part of the script. It's even best to suffer this early because it is only making you stronger.

1. *What are the lifestyles will you adopt today to build a strong foundation for success?*

____

____

____

____

____

____

____

2. *What are your limitations to attaining a strong foundation to succeed?*

____

____

3. *Put down twenty life event that happened to you today that you are you grateful.*

4. *What habits are limiting you from achieving greater heights in your goal?*

Behavior 6: Stop Allowing Them To Talk You Out Of It

Influence is good, but it becomes bad when it is not checked. What I mean is, it's a great thing when the person who have your interest at heart is influencing you on something that will do you a lot of good and not someone with a stray opinion. It's wise to sieve advices every given time.

Many people have a way with words, they can break all the work you have put towards achieving your goal in one meeting, so all that hard work, the diet you have sustained for months, the weight you have successfully dropped, the drive to return back to studies... all died after one meeting with the devil. You all know I really don't mean the devil. But it is painful, to attain so much gain and someone just comes and crashes the entire process. Anyway like I always say, only I can give anyone the permission to ruin my life.

It's become a heavyweight when the people who supported your dream begin to dwindle and that starts to affect the greater part of you. It starts small and then the discomfort your dream is causing begins to show and then you start to think if this was your goal in the first place. There is no reason to feel guilty, we are human and emotions are bound to rise sometimes. Like I have mentioned time and time again, resolving to take up your dream and run will not go down well with many people you care about. Suddenly you become scares, your hangout time with your friends reduces, and even your spouse hardly gets to see enough of you... This is beyond your control girl, don't feel down. All of the heartbreak you are experiencing as regards to this stride you have decided to take comes with the full package, although a lot were never prepared for it.

Let's pause for a second? On the subject of someone being inconvenienced by a person's pursuit for success, how can you bring them to see things from your mind eyes? Being inconvenienced is part of life and any relationship, One thing I know that works is for you to be able to change another person's life; you have to change yours first. People don't change because you force them to, they change because they are inspired by your life. There is no magic here, the change starts with you; build up enough courage and resolve to work on yourself and don't bother about the inconveniences your success journey is causing them for with time they will not be called inconveniences anymore but examples, principles, and values to adopt.

No matter how heavy the pressure gets, don't go back on your dreams. They feel you are getting proud, shutting them out, leaving them behind... They are not in the same race as you and I don't understand, so they can't call the shots. Sometimes it's share insecurity and fear that's causing the lack of support, don't be discouraged; instead double your efforts at attaining your goal, it's not your duty to take them up the ladder with you so they can see the light, but it's your duty to account for your own dreams. So, fight for yourself...

You cannot control what they will say, how they will think or react to your dream, but you can control yours which is most important here. So instead of distancing yourself from all the negative comments and staying away from your loved ones and causing a war, here are some of the things you can adapt to help you better control your reactions.

Ask yourself, is the person supposed to even be in your life in the first place? Because seriously; if you are not here to make me a better person, then we need to reconsider this relationship. I'm sure you have inconvenienced yourself for these set of people a number of times, so why can't they do the same for you?

Be intentional about seeing them and speak to them on the matter. Go to them physically prepared and positive that the outcome of the meeting will be fruitful. Have the answers to their questions already prepared in your mind. Remind yourself why you are doing this and why it matters so much.

LESSON

Intentionally plan to make it easier on your loved ones. Don't just throw your dreams in their faces and disappear. Make plans in retrospect, be a proactive woman. Draw up a calendar that has it all together, this way even if any guilt wants to slip by your heart, you know you have managed the issue and you are more motivated than worried about the inconveniences that are beyond your control. At the end of the day, we all will be alright.

1. *How did you deal with the pressure and complaint while attempting your dreams?*

___

___

___

___

___

___

___

___

___

___

2. *How do you think you can deal with an obstinate loved one who is nagging so much about being inconvenienced be your goal pursuit?*

____

____

____

____

____

____

____

____

3. *How do you think you can get people in your life that matter to be more supportive of your dream?*

____

____

____

____

____

____

____

____

____

Behavior 7: Learn To Say No

Are you in charge of your will? Or you are still of the "I care what people's opinion is about me" school of thought and so I'm bent on pleasing them all. You should know that it is okay to say no to things if it's not going down well with you. Don't be a mannequin that everyone toys with, have a mind of your own it's not a sin. If an offer comes for you to do something presents itself, if it's not going down well in your guts; simply say NO.

LESSON

In any situation, you find yourself in life, wade off the opinions and approval of others and do what you are at peace with. Everything cannot be equally as important as the others, if not then none of them is important. So, learn to say NO without any iota of guilt. Don't forget to respond as soon as possible so your silence is not misinterpreted, so say it as it is very politely but firmly.

1. *Have you successfully learned to say no yet?*

____

____

____

____

____

____

____

____

2. *Do you feel you need to?*

____

____

____

3. *If you were to advise us on more effective ways to say NO asides the practices above, what will that be?*

PART III: SKILLS TO ACQUIRE

A lot has been said and leaving out this aspect will weaken the strong structure we have been trying to build since. Skill is the enablement to do something well and attain expertise in our given field.

Skills are learned abilities. No one is born unique or with special abilities. For every great stride anyone achieves, there is a high level of focus, time dedicated and hard work.

Skill 1: Planning

There is a popular saying that goes "If you fail to plan, then you have planned to fail". So failing to plan is also planning but for failure this time. Not making a plan will evade your focus even if you had a great dream and frustrate the entire process.

The first thing you need to know about achieving your goal is to be fully convinced of where you are headed. Don't be amongst those who claim to know it all, even a map is only useful if you know the workings of both the end and the beginning. Meaning for you to start off to reach your end game, you should know where you are if not you will not get to where you want to go.

What do you have listed out in your road map strategy? What is your starting point? And what is your finish line? What is your plan of attack when the need arises? Think your plan through meticulously, brainstorm, you can even gather trusted friends to assist in guiding you aright. You can't get lost if you know where you are going to, it's that simple. The idea here is so that you get to your destination faster and competently. Don't plan your destination on your way to the uncertain destination, plan your destination before you even embark on the destination.

Starting with the finished line and focused on one goal. Yes, you are wondering if that's correct, it is. By this time and at this point you should already know how your end will be, so; start at the end. This strategy has always been effective and productive because it clearly displays the direction your path should go.

Now you are aware of where you are going to, it will be easy to trace back to where you ought to start from. What are the resources you need to carry out this function, what arsenals do you need to be fully equipped with? Do you need to learn about the terrain you are about to tread on? Do you need skills to project your best self? What habits should I drop and which new ones am I to pick up? What and what do I have to improve on? Be totally honest with yourself and get all you need and then get to work.

With a clear picture of the end and the starting point, you need to be strong in the middle as well. A deep thinking session will pay off here to get your guideposts in place (don't have too much so you are not clogged up). Here just write down whatever comes to your head, don't think if you are even making sense; later on, it will come together. Ask all the questions you have residing in your heart and get to honestly answer them too. Aim to get better and evolve every day as you are on this journey, don't be comfortable with knowing the much you know, surge forward and learn some more. Know how to do one thing 10 different ways.

Your guidepost contains your real possibility list and everything that will help you grow along the way. This is not as easy as it sounds; the road map you have planned is not going to supernaturally make your journey stress-free, it's only to give your journey a focus and direction.

LESSON

Not making plans drains and wastes the time and effort you would have put into acquiring your goals more sooner. Not mapping out your own plan to follow to acquire your dreams opens you up to adopting someone else's dream you have no business with as your own because it seems like a great dream.

1. *What will your road map strategy look like, let's see your progress.*

___

___

___

___

___

2. *Are you of the habit of embarking on a goal and not planning effectively for it?*

3. *Have you ever tried the strategy of planning discussed above, if yes; how did it turn out?*

4. *What skills do you want to acquire now that will help achieve your goals?*

Skill 2: Confidence

Not many know this, but confidence is a skill because it can be improved on. It's not inborn, it can be inculcated as we grow up and further developed as we mature but it is a virtue everyone needs to pursue.

Here are some key areas that needs to be addressed to regain our confidence; first it's our appearance, how do you look. Many women get married and feel that's the last and greatest achievement they can ever have in life. They let go of the prim and proper self they used to be, they don't take proper care of their hair, fingernails, toenails, personal hygiene, teeth, breath... There are just a lot to mention here, you all know the rest. I love to makeup and I do it; not because the world wants me to look in a type of way but because it makes me feel great and when I feel great I am confident. Let's get this straight, I'm not confident because of the makeup I have on, but because I like the way I look. Have you ever come across a woman who doesn't feel great and confident when she looks great? If you have, I haven't in all my years on earth and touring the world.

What is that personal style (dress sense) of yours that helps you rock your confidence better? Get your game on and always look on point! This is not about being materialistic at all, confidence gained from wearing your best self-look is drawn from learning how to look the part of a confident woman. I said best self-look because I am directing your attention to adopting your own look and not someone else's look. Loving the way you look is a great feeling, you think about it. Anytime it is hair day, or pedicure and manicure day, or you are being adorned up for a big occasion, don't you feel very special? That's the idea here, don't appear to any function looking just anyhow, always looking the part at all times.

How do you act? Form a habit of always acting confident even when you don't have any idea of what the subject matter is. When you are approached as a woman on a subject matter, don't flag it off immediately and say you know anything about it. Speak from an enlightened place and research on it later. I always advise people to read wide, read anything you come across, soccer, fashion, engineering, music, management... anything at all; this way you may never get stuck in a conversation. A lot of good comes from acting confident even when you are not. Lastly, confidence as mentioned earlier can be groomed. Be around friends that have a high confidence level in themselves and you will be confident. Be careful the friends you hang around with, what are they instilling in you, what are you hearing? Generally, change your perception of life today; you can only get out of life what you invest in it.

LESSON

Confidence is very important in reaching your set goals; the fact that you have a low-confidence level doesn't make it a lost situation. Start to improve your confidence level in all areas you feel vulnerable in and be your best-self going forward.

1. *What do you feel you need to change or improve on about your appearance to boost your confidence and how do you intend to go about it?*

____

____

____

____

2. *Talking about acting confident in the face of being void of a subject matter presented to you, have you ever found yourself in that situation and how did you handle it?*

3. *Do you think your friends have negatively affected your confidence level and would you retain or change your group of friends today?*

Skill 3: Persistence

I believe nothing good in life comes easy. Persistence is what differentiates an achiever from a bearer of a myriad of excuses. I never said attaining your dream will come very quick nor did I say it is easy, it will drain you, it will push you to the wall and you will almost give up. Only dogged people make head way in life, but everyone's timing is different. Don't mix this up please, because "A" got to her destination in the space of six months doesn't mean you will use the same timeframe as well. You may reach your desired end earlier or much later than the aforementioned individual. We are all different people, and our timing on earth is equally different.

Don't be intimidated by their success, you are only at your starting point and you are here feeling down for someone's middle. It's a very wrong notion to give your goal an end date. You can have your mile indicators with dates to tell you how productive and efficient you are getting. Discouragements may come, but don't let it weigh you down one bit. It's important you always stand up when you are knocked down, you may not have it all together, but with patience and determination, your resolve will get you home.

LESSON

Ditch the mindset of "what will be, will be", here you have to fight to survive; you have to fight to attain the height you desire. See your goal as a long-term goal and you will keep striving to attain and grow it. Achievers never stop, after attaining this goal, they go on to the next and the next and the one after that. Let patience guide you, let perseverance be your watchword and let persistence be your bedrock.

1. *Tell your story of how persistent you were in pursuing your dreams.*

____
____
____
____
____
____
____
____
____

2. *Do you think persistence is enough to help you be patient in acquiring your goals?*

____
____
____
____
____
____
____
____
____

Skill 4: Effectiveness

It is very easy to get distracted these days. While you think you are in the perfect will of your dreams, you have been able to create time to pursue it squarely; whereas all you needed was to use that time more impactful. Here is how to be highly productive as you walk this walk.

Exchange your to-do-list with a results-list. You have to be intentionally result oriented and not just for the fun of crossing out items on the list. By the way, what do you have in the list, what have you crossed out so far? Are they mighty feats or the easiest ones every dick, tom and harry can handle? You have filled up your to-do-list with irrelevant items again. Are those items you are crossing out bringing you closer to your mile marker? A results-list seeks end results, instead of writing up to-do-lists; put down action points on ways to tackle the challenge you are faced with. To-do-lists can be very vague at times, with a lot of things but no measure to take to handle it.

Secondly, rethink your competence. Bring your competence/productivity level to the drawing board and let's re-evaluate it. Yes, you are achieving results, but you can do better than what you have now. Hard work is good but coupled with smartness is great. Don't remain in that comfort zone, think of more ways to improve at what you are doing and double your result rate.

A productive atmosphere is a must have. The right environment can put you so in the mood that you will be shocked at the level of result you will get afterwards. By now you should know what works for you. Is your productive environment amongst wildlife (in a cage though)? Are you most inspired when you are on a vacation on a beautiful island? Is it amongst live flowers and the natural scents help to clear the clogged brain? What works for you?

Take off anything that will distract you like your cell phone, or an attractive cup with write-ups all over it. It's different things for different people. What stands as a distraction for you should go away completely so you can get the job done. Very often, check on your work/dream. Ask yourself am I still on the right track? What have I attained? Do a self-audit on your dream and trust me you will regain your focus if you have derailed.

LESSON

Don't stop at setting aside time to work on your goals and work to achieve the right things.

1. *How often do you make a to-do-lists and do you now understand the concept of results-list?*

____
____
____
____
____
____

2. *What is your efficiency level and what ways will you improve on it?*

3. *What atmosphere works for you and makes you very productive?*

Skill 5: Positivity

What's your attitude to life? When you are faced with a quagmire situation, how do you react? When the situation is very horrible, do you throw in the towel and let the challenge win? There can be very terrible situations in life that the best option is to give in to the problem. But look up, in the midst of this predicament; can you find any positive light? Do you know you can choose your attitude, mindset and focus in every situation you find yourself? This is what differentiates joy from suffering.

Imagine the worse situation you ever found yourself in, you will discover that tiny light at the end of the tunnel no matter how dark it looks. So, you see; your approach to situations is largely affected by your mindset.

LESSON

You cannot control the situations you are faced with but you can control how you react to it.

1. *How do you approach issues when faced with challenges?*

____

____

____

____

____

____

____

____

____

2. *Would you say you have a positive mindset and how do you know that?*

____

____

____

____

____

____

____

____

Skill 6: Lead-Her-Ship

Leadership is not a trait commonly cheered for females. When the males lead its admired while when women lead it's seen as bossy and not in a woman's place. No wonder we still struggle with the function now. Regardless of whatever you do, you are a leader. Begin to live purposefully, be a source of impact and influence the other woman by your side. Tell her how she deserves a chance to be what she is meant to be, speak truth into her life. I'm sure you know that before you can reach out to another in this manner, you first must have gotten it right.

It will take so much work for only one woman to positively affect the lives of millions; but with joint efforts from many women like you reading this, we can have a stronger effect, so please do your own quota and liberate your world. Pursue your goals, carry others along as you climb (that's what leaders do) and celebrate each other's achievements as you go having in mind that when one of us succeeds, we all have succeeded. There is that magic resident in all of you, this I know for a fact. Let you light shine, don't lock your dreams away; you will discover that you have lighted the way for many more women to replicate this liberation message.

LESSON

Leaders are pacesetters; we make it easy for the coming generation. We have already made all the mistakes they would have made; theirs is just to replicate the legacy.

1. *Would you consider yourself a leader and give instances where you have displayed your leadership skills*

2. *Would you impact your world from today and how do you intend to begin (write down the things you will do)?*

Conclusion

Believe In Yourself

By now I'm sure you are already fired-up to take over your world and dust off that abandoned dream you've left stagnant for years. Allow me to reiterate again; believe in yourself. I don't know how much I can emphasize this. Don't push this piece after reading this last chapter, inculcate the habit of going back to check on the action points you have agreed to adopt above and don't lose sight of them. Let this be part of your daily routine. You are in total control of your life and can do anything you set out to do.

I am positive you will take this and run far with it because I believe in you. Remember, when it gets ugly I won't be there to encourage you, when you are exhausted and about to throw in the towel I will not be there either, when you feel your dream is bigger than you and you are close to giving in to the pressure from friends, family, and colleagues; I am not going to be around you. Recall, I said "WHEN" because it will surely happen.

Darling, you have absolute control of your life; so fight for it. It's as complicated and easy as that. I never said this will be easy, but I said it's bound to make a better you. Don't apologize for the race and who is affected by it, enough of the apologizing. Anyone who cannot take the heat shouldn't be close to the fire. Be kind to yourself but push yourself at the same time. Remember, it isn't easy; but it's worth it. I love you all and see you all at the top.

Recommended Books

Girl, Stop Apologizing: A Shame-Free Plan for Embracing and Achieving Your Goals By Rachel Hollis

Get it Here>> https://www.amazon.com/Girl-Stop-Apologizing-Shame-Free-Embracing/dp/1400209609

You are a Badass Workbook >> ISBN: 1950171868

WORKBOOK for The Longevity Paradox>> ISBN: 1950171795

A JOURNAL For Becoming | A Gratitude & Self Journal (Becoming By Michelle Obama Quotes)>> ISBN: 1098520211

A JOURNAL For Daring Greatly>> ISBN: 195017185X

A Journal The Subtle Art of Not Giving a F*ck>> ISBN: 1950171833

WORKBOOK for The Subtle Art of Not Giving A F*ck >> ISBN: 1950171779

WORKBOOK for Dare to Lead By Brene Brown >> ISBN: 1950171973

Workbook For Daring Greatly>>ISBN: 1950171906

Workbook For How To Win Friends and Influence People>> ISBN: 1950171892

Made in the USA
Monee, IL
12 July 2020

36471610R00046